GARFIELD
Big Fat
Book of Jokes
and Riddles

Based on characters created by Jim Davis
Written by Katy Hall
Illustrated by Mike Fentz

Random House New York

On the right of me was a lion! On the left were two wild elephants! Behind me was a tiger! I was on my trusty steed, going as fast as I could, when all of a sudden . . . the ride stopped and I got off the merry-go-round!

When is Garfield most likely to go into a restaurant?

When the door is open!

What is Garfield's favorite way to catch a fish?

Have someone throw it to him.

Dear Garfield:
  Can you tell me when lilac time is?
                Flower Child

Dear Flower:
  Lilac time is usually the next morning. For example, if someone asks you if you know what happened to a couple of trays of lasagna, you lilac crazy!

Garfield says:

Skiing has brought happiness to many people, and most of them are doctors.

What would you get if you crossed Garfield with a boxer?

A new heavyweight champ!

What would Garfield get if he crossed his pasta with a boa constrictor?

Spaghetti that winds itself around his fork.

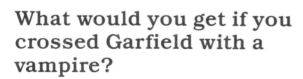

What would you get if you crossed Garfield with a vampire?

A big, furry monster that sucks the tomato sauce out of lasagna.

Dear Garfield:
    I'm writing to you as a cat, since all cats know so much about mice. I want to know, is it true that mice always walk single file?

Moustified

Dear Mouse:
    The one I know does.

Garfield Says:

Odie is *so* dumb! The other day he told me he
was really glad that Jon had named him Odie.
When I asked him why, he said, "'Cause that's
what everybody always calls me."

Garfield asks:

Have you heard about the new method for improving the flavor of salt? Just sprinkle it lightly on a tray of lasagna and eat!

I'm really a very domestic cat. I like to putter around . . . and fix things around the house.

Like big fat sandwiches!

What kind of a bath can Garfield take without water?

A sun bath!

Garfield says:

There are two things I'll never eat for breakfast. Lunch and dinner.

Dear Garfield:
    I'm afraid that I'm losing my memory. What should I do about it?
                    No Elephant

Dear No:
    Try to forget about the problem.

Dear Garfield:
    You never seem to age. I wonder if you can tell me how I could avoid getting wrinkles?

                    Youthful

Dear Youth:
    Don't sleep in your clothes.

Garfield's Definitions:

Menu: A list of dishes that a restaurant has just run out of.

Garfield's Definitions:

Ignorance is when you don't know something and someone finds out.

Why is Garfield called a sound sleeper?

Because he snores!

What time would it be if you saw a dozen German shepherds chasing Garfield up a tree?

Twelve after one!

What did Odie say when he sat
on the sandpaper?

"Ruff! Ruff!"

Garfield's Definitions:

Etiquette: Yawning with your mouth closed.

Dear Garfield:
    Is it good manners to answer a question with just a single word?

                Polite

Dear Polite:
    No.

Dear Garfield:
  I love to cook breakfast for my friends. Is it proper for me to cook it in my pajamas?

            Wondering

Dear Wondering:
  It's not improper, but it can be a big mess. Try a frying pan.

Garfield asks:

Did you hear about the cat who swallowed the ball of yarn? She had six mittens!

Is Garfield a light sleeper?

No! He sleeps in the dark.

What's one bone that Odie can't chew?
A trombone!

Why did Odie wear a winter coat to the baseball game?
He heard that thousands of fans would be there!

Why does Garfield think that Odie's never tasted noodle soup?
Because it's brain food!

My father tipped the scales at 98 pounds. My mother was no featherweight herself. . . . What can I do? I'm just following in their fatsteps.

When is Garfield's mind like a rumpled bed?

When it hasn't been made up yet.

Dear Garfield:
  My teacher says that cats have nine lives. Is there any animal with more lives than that?
                    Curious

Dear Curious:
  Yes, the frog. It croaks every night!

Dear Garfield:
  I have a ringing in my ears. What should I do?
                    Ringo

Dear Ringo:
  Have you considered getting an unlisted ear?

Garfield says:

Dog who puts face in punch bowl . . . gets punch in the nose!

Garfield says:

Jon and I have a give-and-take relationship.
He gives and I take.

How does Garfield feel when he's near a hamburger?

He relishes every moment.

How does Garfield eat an ice cream cone?

Lickity-split.

Why doesn't Garfield ever swim on an empty stomach?

Because it's easier to swim in water!

What question can Garfield never answer "yes" to?

Are you asleep?

Dear Garfield:
   I specialize in astrological charts and I would like to do yours. Can you tell me what sign you were born under?
                   Star Gazer

Dear Star:
   Well, let's see. I think it was under the No Smoking sign in the kitchen of a fine restaurant.

Garfield says:

Talk about dumb! Odie is so dumb, he thinks that a quarterback is a refund!

Garfield asks:

Who put quicksand in the hourglass of time?

Garfield says:

Fat is nature's way of explaining why Jon's grocery bill is $150 a week.

Dear Garfield:
   Can you tell me where hippos are found?
   Animal Lover

Dear Animal:
   Hippos are so big that they hardly ever get lost.

Dear Garfield:
   What's the best way to keep leftover lasagna?
   Thrifty

Dear Thrifty:
   Simply don't give any of it back.

Garfield's Definitions:

Stakeout: What Jon says at the supermarket when he sees the price of beef.

SHOW ME A VOICE CRYING IN THE WILDERNESS... AND I'LL SHOW YOU A CAMPER WHO FORGOT THE LASAGNA.

Why was Garfield standing in front of the mirror with his eyes closed?

He wanted to see what he looked like when he was asleep.

How is Garfield like a turkey?

They both gobble.

Can Garfield jump higher than a footstool?

Of course! A footstool can't jump.

Yippiiiiiii!!!

If Garfield had wings, what would he be?

A jumbo jet.

Is Garfield a good dancer?

No! He's got two left feet.

Garfield's favorite Shakespearean quote:

Tubby or not tubby, that is the question!

What does Garfield consider a hair-raising experience?
Taking off a turtleneck sweater.

What kind of tree is Garfield's favorite?

The pantry.

What kind of bird does Garfield like best?

The swallow.

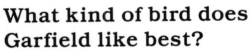

What flowers grow between Garfield's nose and chin?

His tulips.

Dear Garfield:
   I'd like to know how to avoid getting that rundown feeling.
                         Tired

Dear Tired:
   Look both ways before you cross the street.

Dear Garfield:
   I am going to climb the Rockies this summer. What should I use to cook my food?
                         Camper

Dear Camp:
   A mountain range, what else?

If Garfield has six roast chickens and Odie asks
for one, how many will Garfield have left?

Six!

REMEMBER THE À LA MODE!

Dear Garfield:
   I would like to teach my cat a few simple tricks. Is there anything I should know first?
                     Stumped

Dear Stumped:
   More than the cat!

Garfield says:

Vacations are really stupid. You get in the car and drive for days looking for a good home-cooked meal!

Garfield's Definitions:

Ringleader: The first one into the bathtub!

If Garfield smashed his alarm clock, could he be accused of killing time?

Not if the clock struck first!

How long does it take Garfield to eat dinner?

Oh, Garfield usually takes two or three seconds.

What is Garfield's favorite tourist attraction?

The Great Gorge!

GARFIELD, I HAD A DREAM LAST NIGHT THAT YOU EXPLODED FROM EATING TOO MANY PANCAKES.

HOW WAFFLE!

Dear Garfield:
    My father is very proud of his looks, but recently his hair has started to fall out. What's the best thing to keep it in?
                        Sonny

Dear Sonny:
    A paper bag.

If Garfield got a job working for Liz the vet, what would you call him?

A first-aid kit.

When is Garfield not a cat?

When he walks down the street and turns into a restaurant.

When Garfield sits on a fence, how is he like a quarter?

Head's on one side and tail's on the other.

Garfield says:

Odie is so dumb! He thinks a big-game hunter is someone who's trying to find out where the World Series is being played!

Garfield says:

I do my hardest work before breakfast—getting up.

What did Jon say when he couldn't find Odie?

"Doggone!"

What seven letters did Garfield say when he opened the refrigerator and saw that there was nothing to eat?

O I C U R M T

What did Garfield have to pay when he was picked up for hitchhiking?

Thumb tax.

Why did Garfield pack a 100-watt
bulb in his lunch box?

He wanted a light snack.

If Odie has a whole chicken and Garfield only has a bite, what should he do?

Scratch it!

What's the most stirring book Garfield can read?

A cookbook!

What would you get if you crossed Odie with a rose?

A bloomin' idiot!

What would Garfield win if he went on a diet and lost 25 pounds?

The No Belly Prize!

How does Garfield dress on a freezing cold day?

Quickly!

If Garfield orders bison steak
at a restaurant, what does the
waiter bring him after the meal?

The buffalo bill!

Garfield's Definitions:

Heroes: What Garfield does when he gets into a boat.

Why does Odie wag his tail?

Because no one else will wag it for him.

How many legs does Odie have if you call his tail a leg?

Four! Even if you call a tail a leg, it's still a tail.

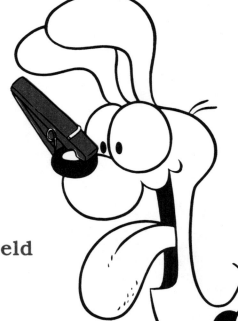

What's the best way for Garfield to keep Odie from smelling?

Hold his nose.

YOU PROBABLY DIDN'T KNOW ODIE WAS A POLICE DOG. SURE, HE DOESN'T LOOK LIKE ONE. THAT'S BECAUSE HE'S IN THE SECRET SERVICE.

What did Liz call Garfield's small scratch?

A short cut!

Dear Garfield:
  Please tell me the best cure for insomnia.
  Restless

Dear Restless:
  A good night's sleep!

When traveling in space, what would Garfield's favorite meal be?

Launch.

If athletes get athlete's foot, what might Garfield the astronaut get?

Missile toe!

Why didn't Garfield want to try the new restaurant on the moon?

He heard it didn't have any atmosphere.

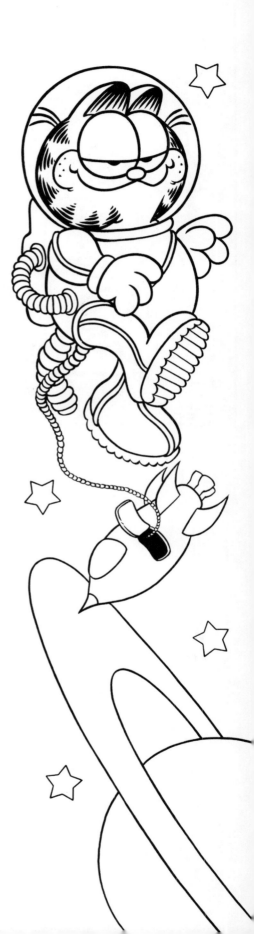

Why did Garfield want to travel by railroad?

He heard it was a chew-chew train!

Garfield's Definitions:

Oatmeal: What to serve when an oat comes to dinner.

Garfield's Definitions:

Laplander: Someone who can't keep his balance while riding on a bus.

Garfield says:

Odie is so stupid! If he went shopping for a color TV, he wouldn't know which color to buy!

Garfield says:

You know you're too thin when . . . you have to run around in the shower to get wet!

Dear Garfield:
I've been studying history, but there's one thing I can't figure out. Why did Robin Hood rob only the rich?

Puzzled

Dear Puzzled:
Because the poor had no money!

Dear Garfield:
I want to do well on my history test tomorrow, so I wonder if you could tell me where the Declaration of Independence was signed?

Polly Sigh

Dear Pol:
At the bottom.

Why did Garfield take a hammer to bed with him?

So he could hit the hay!

It must take a lot of practice to be such a perfect idiot!

Garfield says:

I don't believe in eating on an empty stomach!

Why is Garfield's nose in the middle of his face?

Because it's the scenter.

What did Garfield's right ear say to his left ear?

Do you live on this block too?

Why doesn't Garfield use toothpaste?

Because none of his teeth are loose.

Garfield's Definitions:

Synonym: The word you use when you can't spell the other one.

What would you get if you crossed Garfield with a canary?

A cat that's not hungry anymore!

Garfield asks:

Did you hear about the crook who went around stealing people's false teeth? He was operating a big teething ring!

Which has more legs, a cat or no cat?

No cat. A cat has four legs but no cat has eight legs!

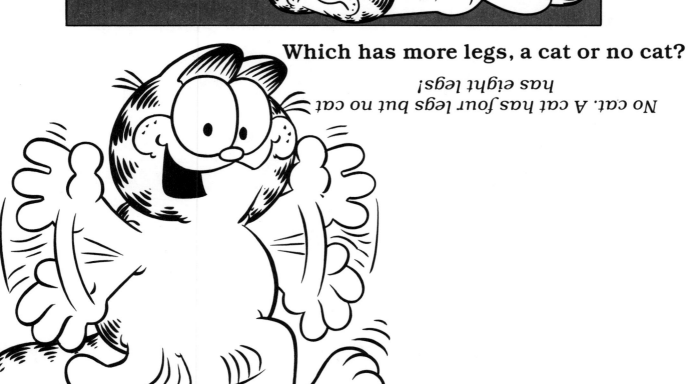

In what month does Garfield eat the least?

February—it's the shortest month.

Why wouldn't Garfield ever starve if he was lost in the desert?

Because he could eat the sand which is there.

What looks like half a tray of lasagna?

The other half.

Garfield says:

You know you're too fat when . . .
your friends say, "Pull up a sofa and sit down."

Garfield's Definitions:

Dieting: The triumph of mind over platter.

Dear Garfield:
   I wonder if you can tell me how many famous men were born in New York City?
   City Boy

Dear City Boy:
   None! Only babies are born there!

Why does Garfield go to bed?

Because his bed won't come to him.

What kind of music would Garfield compose while in bed?

Sheet music!

What kind of detective would Garfield be?

An undercover agent.

Garfield's Definitions:

Waffle: A pancake with nonstick treads.

Dear Garfield:
   I'd like to know what the difference is between a tuna fish and a piano.
                    Eager to Learn

Dear Eager:
   It's simple. You can always tune a piano, but you can't tune a fish.

**What does Garfield call it
when Odie has a brainstorm?**

Drizzle.

What does Odie drink while he's watching a boxing match?

Punch!

How did Odie spend last Thursday

Who can spend Thursday?
You need money!

What did Odie say when Garfield grabbed him by the tail?

"This is the end of me!"

Garfield's Definitions:

Thanksgiving dinner:
The pause that refleshes!

Garfield says:

I used to have 45-inch hips until
I started drinking low-fat milk.
Talk about low fat . . . now I have
45-inch ankles!

Dear Garfield:
   I'm studying geography and I wondered if you could tell me where potatoes were first found.
                              Student

Dear Stu:
   In the ground.

Dear Garfield:
   How can you tell a pine tree from a dogwood?
                              Tree Lover

Dear Tree:
   By its bark!

Dear Garfield:
   I've just moved to the coast and met a lot of fisher-men, and what I'd like to know is, why are fishermen so stingy?
                              Land Lubber

Dear Land:
   Their job makes them sell fish!

Why did Odie stand behind the donkey?

He thought he'd get a kick out of it!

Garfield says:

Never stick your head in the oven . . . unless you're looking for a baked bean.

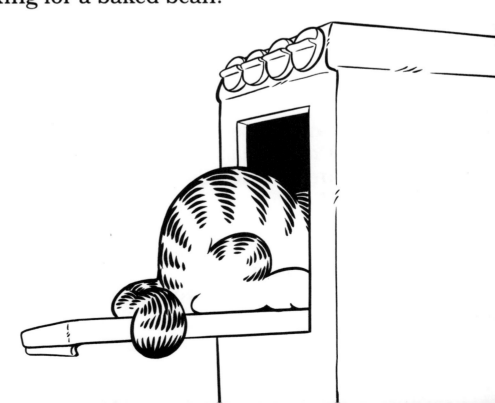

Dear Garfield:
   I'm about 50 pounds underweight. What I want to know is, what's the best way to get fat?

Skinny

Dear Skinny:
   The best way to get fat is from the butcher!

What's the easiest breakfast for Garfield to have in bed?

A couple of rolls.

What happened to Garfield when he swallowed three bullets?

His fur grew out in bangs!

If Jon gave 5 cents to Garfield and 20 cents to Odie, what time would it be?

A quarter to two!

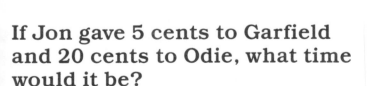

Garfield's Definitions:

Bread: Raw toast.

Garfield asks:

Do you know why a banana can't stay out in the sun too long?

Because a banana peels!

Why doesn't Garfield like tennis balls?

Because you can serve them but you can't eat them!

Why did Garfield stop eating the giant doughnut?

He got tired of the hole thing!

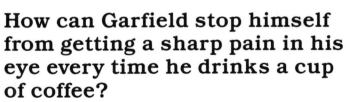

What did Garfield say to the lollipop?

"I can lick you any day!"

How can Garfield stop himself from getting a sharp pain in his eye every time he drinks a cup of coffee?

He can take the spoon out of the cup!

What can a bird do that Garfield can't?

Take a bath in a saucer!

Garfield asks:

What's worse than a karate chop in the chest?

A week-old pork chop in the stomach!

What did Garfield get when he accidentally sat down on the stove burner?

Rump roast!

Why did Garfield comb his hair before he went to bed?

He wanted to make a good impression on his pillow.

If Garfield wakes up thirsty in the middle of the night, what should he do?

Lift up the mattress and find the spring!

Why did Liz get a private hospital bed for Garfield?

Because he was too cute for wards!

What is just as big as Garfield, but doesn't weigh a single pound?

Garfield's shadow!